# The Medit  diet

# meal plan

Mediterranean Diet Food Plan: Your Complete Plan to Harness the Power of the Healthiest Diet on the Planet, Lose Weight, Prevent Heart Disease and More

# Table of Contents

# Introduction

The Mediterranean basin is the cradle of civilization – Rome and its glory, Greece in its grandeur, wizened old Egypt and the Levant. These great conquerors and statesman treaded across the world with their accomplishments, and the imprint left in our collective conscious is still greater. King Tutankhamen, Pythagoras, and Julius Caesar are names known to all, with Pythagoras earning the ire of middle schoolers the world over with his triangle math. But with their culture and influence, they also brought a second very distinct item – their food. The Mediterranean is also the home to one of the healthiest diets in the world, the creatively-named Mediterranean diet. In 2010, it received the accolade of UNESCO's World Heritage designation, placing it in a pantheon of cultural monoliths like Stonehenge and the Acropolis.

When the Romans stomped across all known civilization and beyond, to the lands that would support it, they brought three crops vital to Roman and wider Mediterranean civilization namely the grape, wheat, and the olive. Obviously, they didn't bring them everywhere - the marshy swamps of yet-mature Germany wouldn't work, nor remote and rocky Britain, but theirs. The Greek and Phoenician influence are why all the land that touches the Mediterranean is known for its bountiful and flavorful varieties of bread, olive oil, and wine. There's one more essential component, however.

You may have noticed a few things in your life – one that the Mediterranean is an ocean, and oceans are made of water, and fish – get this – live in water. The piece of our dietary puzzle? Fish. These people ate tons of it. Romans made a sauce of fermented anchovies that Italians still make to this day. Such was the depth of their devotion to consuming this animal. Fish was plentiful for them, and its incredible health benefits are what really seal this diet in as a potent tool for improving health. This book attempts to give you a thorough tour of the Mediterranean diet; a more in-depth look at its history, health benefits, and some recipes to get you started.

### How strict do I have to be?

Managing cravings is a big part of being on a diet, and for many people, it can be the hardest part, too. While changing what you eat on a day-to-day basis is one thing, when social pressures are mixed in, and possibly alcohol, inhibitions lower. There's a reason why the phenomena of "peer pressure" exists – because it's a powerful tool in modulating behavior. Seeing your friends binge and eat five desserts each will make you want to do it, too. This is probably a big reason why diets fail. You aren't sure what's appropriate and what's not, and in what quantities. The answer to how strict to be when you go out is in no way an easy one and is controlled by dozens of different factors in your life. The second half of this chapter is about knowing when you can get a little loose with your eating, and when you should reel it in, and ways to avoid temptations and keep yourself under control.

Remember back at the beginning of the book? We had talked about your goals - why are you on this diet, what do you hope to accomplish? Weight loss, reducing the chance of a disease, athletic performance? Think of where you are right now, where you want to be, and how close you are. Your genes and past behavior also play a huge role. If your older relatives look at a piece of cake and gain a pound, the same biology is probably present in you. Past behavior as well – are you prone to binging or can you control yourself? Psychologically stable people usually have an easier time controlling themselves, so making sure that you don't use food as an emotional crutch is a big aspect. Finally, there's your activity level – while fit people generally have greater discipline, they also have a little more wiggle room when it comes to indulgences, as long as it's not happening every night.

## Goals

Let's get one thing straightened out right now. If weight loss is your primary goal, there really is no way around the simple and firm tenet that indulging will set you back, no matter how infrequently. This does mean never indulge, the opposite in fact. Some indulgences are good for you, because if you continually refuse the idea of it, and one day you break, you break that much worse. It's better to go out with your friends and have a few drinks and journey outside your dietary zone a few times a month than it is to save it all up in one session and binge drink and eat. Binge drinking and eating is shocking to the body and can result in serious long-term damage if you're not careful. An occasional indulgence will help curb your appetite for them in the long run – they'll seem like special treats as opposed to dire and gnawing needs.

Say your goal is something a little more unconventional, at least when dieting is concerned. Say you're trying to put on weight for a sport you play because you're not strong enough or need to change weight classes. If you've been following and maintaining your diet very well so far, a little indulgence may actually do you some good, because the extra calories would help fuel the recovery you so desperately need to change your body composition. Of course, considering what to order is important too – this is not an excuse to bulk up on ice cream, but usually, restaurant food is richer than what we're used to eating at home, but skimping on alcohol is recommended as alcohol can interfere with recovery, resting, and synthesis of new muscle tissue. Activity level and having a higher muscle mass will inherently raise your need for more calories in the first place, with people with a higher muscle mass having a higher basal metabolic rate – the calories you burn just existing – than an untrained person.

Lastly, if you're being called out on the town and you're mostly looking to avoid certain diseases, this is where some research needs to get done. It depends on what you think you might be prone to – heart disease would necessitate that you avoid any saturated fat when you go out, and especially trans fat. Diabetes might mean you've got to skip on dessert. One of the few uniting factors of all these sorts of different lifestyle diseases is inflammation, though. If you eat a diet that is prone to reducing it, it will help you across the board with avoiding things like heart disease, cancer, and diabetes. For considerations of anti-inflammatory foods, think some of the most common food in the diet – leafy green vegetables and fish. Try to find those on the diet, and remember to ask where the fish is from!

## Genetics

This is one of the more grim realities of the world – that our genes control much of our health, from our bones to our heart to our metabolism. Some realities are simply impossible to avoid. It may be your family carries extra weight, and always has as far back as you can see, or that your blood sugar may spike unusually high, or you're prone to this or that health problem. Maybe it's the opposite, maybe your natural basal metabolic rate is so high that you can effectively be attached to a feeding tube and gain to no weight, though this is rarely a gift unaccompanied, there is always a price to pay.

Find out what runs in your family, what your health risks are. Alcoholism follows a notoriously sanguineous path, so avoiding drunken shenanigans may be in your best interest if so. If you know you're predisposed to gaining weight, drink water and try to vicariously live through your friends, as anything else carries the risk of extra inches around your waistline.

## Past Behavior

Maybe, this is the best indicator of where you should draw the line when going out. Past behavior is among the top predictors of future behavior – if you've done it before, you'll do it again, and this is where it pays off to know who you really are. Be honest with yourself – if you know that you're capable of blacking out and eating an entire cake without tasting it, avoid the damn cake. Know what you use to comfort you. In the mindfulness section, I mentioned that you need to keep your relationship with food in mind. Make sure you don't use it as a replacement for affection and affirmation from yourself or any others.

## Techniques to keep faith

It's the easiest thing in the world to preach what to do and what not to do, but it's a million times harder to actually do it. Thankfully, behavioral psychology was devised for this exact reason, and there is a slew of mental techniques to retrain your brain in times of weakness.

- **Visualization:** Take advantage of your unique human neurology and really reflect on the long-term consequences of your behavior. What will be the effects of binging with your friends in 5 years; financially, psychologically, socially and physically? Are you capable of living with this future you might create for yourself?

- **Honesty:** This really goes along with the content earlier in this chapter. Don't deny that you're on the diet to lose weight, or that you once drank an entire gallon of wine with a pound of crackers when you were sad. Lying to yourself is a way to rationalize behaviors you know you shouldn't be doing in the first place, and only takes you farther back. Also, ask yourself, is it really worth the splurging?

- **Stay informed:** Know your diet, know your health benefits. Simple things like knowing what you're putting in your body – provided you have the proper nutrition facts and all that, will greatly impact your mind.

- **Make a promise, out loud:** As we said before, in-group shaming is probably one of the most ancient ways we got people to do things we didn't like them doing. Make a point of telling everyone, as you go out, the things you plan to do or not to do. If you violate what you say, everyone can mock you for it, which is an awful feeling. Shame weighs heavier than a lead shawl on your shoulders.

- **Make a plan:** Elaborate on what you intend to do on that night you go out with writing. Make a promise to yourself that you won't go crazy, or that you'll enjoy within reason. Writing down things like that can help dispel anxieties about the night and keep you sharp and focused.

## Eating out the Mediterranean

Overall, eating out on the Mediterranean diet is not challenging, as long as you keep some basic dieting strategies in mind. The diet is not dogmatically restrictive, but it's still recommended to keep some basic nutritional principles and eating strategies in mind when going out to avoid excess empty calories. (I'm looking at you, salad dressing). If you're going to go out and you're thinking of indulging, it's important to know when and how much, and strategies for figuring this out, before you do.

## Chapter 5: Recipes

And here we are at the fun part – the actual food and what to eat. The recipes will be divided into some basic sections – "mother" recipes, a few basic fundamentals, and then breakfast, lunch, and dinner.

## Mother Recipes

There are five things that can be made at home relatively easily that will save you a lot of money in the long run if you want to follow this diet Those five things are a bread, yogurt, a basic tomato sauce, bone stock, and tzatziki sauce.

## Basic Yogurt

(110 kcal, P: 9 gr, Net Carbs: 12 gr, F:  3 gr for six ounces)

This might be your first time fermenting something, and that's fine. All it takes is some patience and a candy thermometer.

### Equipment:

- Candy thermometer
- Stockpot
- Wooden spoon
- Measuring cup

### Ingredients:

- Yogurt culture (Usually, a tablespoon or .5 cup of yogurt is fine)
- Milk (whole milk yogurt used for reference.)

### Directions:

1. In the pot, pour your milk in. Yogurt and milk are a 1:1 ratio – a half gallon of milk makes a half gallon of yogurt. Attach your candy thermometer to the side of the pan and make sure it's immersed in the milk.
2. Gently raise the milk to 200 degrees Fahrenheit, while stirring the entire time. Make sure nothing gets stuck to the bottom and no skin forms on top. If it does, peel it off or break it up into small pieces and mix it back up with the milk.
3. When the milk reaches 200 degrees, turn off the heat and take a half cup of it out in a measuring cup and mix it with the yogurt culture.
4. Then, mix the yogurt-milk mixture back into the warm milk.
5. Cover and store overnight. If you did it right, you should be met with the enzymatic smell of yogurt.

**Recipe ideas:**
1. Use as a marinade, sauce thickener, or by itself with oats and fruit.
2. Strain with cheesecloth to make into Greek yogurt.

## Basic Focaccia Bread

(250 kcal, P: 9, Net Carbs: 36, F: 8, Fi: 2)

Making bread can be intimidating, but it's far easier than it looks. This recipe is almost foolproof, and it's extremely versatile. Just because it's called focaccia doesn't mean it has to be used in Italian food. It's a very simple crusty white bread that goes with many foods and can be seasoned however you want.

**Equipment:**

- Mixing bowl
- Baking pan

**Ingredients:**

- 1.5 cups of warm water (around 110 degrees, a bit hotter than your finger)
- 2.5 cups of flour
- .25 ounce of active-dry yeast
- Teaspoon of honey
- Salt and pepper to taste
- Any seasonings you want
- .25 cup of extra-virgin olive oil

**Directions:**

1. Dissolve your yeast into your water and stir.
2. Pour in your flour, oil, honey, salt, and pepper into your bowl with your water.

3. Mix until you have a warm, soft-but-not-sticky glob.
4. Cover with towel. Leave it in a warm place for an hour or so.
5. If you did it right, it will have risen and swelled up.
6. Take the ball of risen dough and roll it out onto your baking pan, season how you want.
7. Bake at 400 degrees Fahrenheit for 25 minutes or until golden brown

## Basic Tomato sauce

(70 kcal, P: 3 gr, Net Carbs: 16 gr, F: 4 gr, Fi: 4 gr per cup.)
This can be used for pasta, eggs, bread, stews, soups, meats, beans – essentially anything savory you can think of. Its seasoning blend are endemic to the entire Mediterranean, so you can use it no matter what sort of cuisine you're making.

### Equipment:

- Stainless steel pot
- Cutting board
- Knife
- Spoon

### Ingredients:

- Salt and pepper
- 2 tablespoons extra-virgin olive oil
- Oregano
- 1 clove of garlic
- 1 teaspoon of honey
- 32 ounce can of crushed tomatoes

### Directions:

1. Heat oil on medium-low heat and cut garlic. Add to pan when it gets warm.
2. After garlic has browned, add crushed tomatoes, salt, pepper, and oregano to taste, and a spot of honey.
3. Let it simmer for 30 minutes.

**Recipe ideas:**

1. Try eating it with eggs for Mediterranean style fried eggs, known under many different names.
2. It's great with toasted, browned sardines as a dip or a cooking liquid.

## Basic Bone Stock

(Nutrition varies by batch)

This is the basis of many good soups and stews. Bone stock can be made from any animal, pig, chicken, or beef, but the most common are pork and chicken. You can usually find cuts of the beef femur to be used as stock, but pork ribs and chicken skeletons also work great. If you want an extra-rich version, use something like chicken feet or pork trotters. The gelatin leeches out, lending extra body and flavor. If the fat suspended in the broth puts you off, you can put it in the fridge and wait for it to rise to the top. Then, you can simply peel it off.

**Equipment:**

- Stockpot
- Roasting pan
- Knife
- Cutting board

**Ingredients:**

- Salt and pepper
- 1 Tablespoon of olive oil
- 1 clove of garlic
- 1 onion
- 2 ribs of celery
- 3 lb of bones

**Directions:**

1. Preheat oven to 350.
2. Slice vegetables finely, arrange them and the bones on the roasting tray, pour oil and sprinkle with salt and pepper.
3. Roast for 40-50 minutes until browned.
4. Remove pan from oven.
5. Take bones and vegetables and put them in a Stockpot. Fill it with water until covered.
6. Bring to rolling boil, and then reduce to a simmer.
7. Let it simmer for 12-24 hours.

# Tzatziki Sauce

(250 kcal, P: 18 gr, Net Carbs: 6 gr, F: 17 gr per 7 ounces)

The tangy sauce they put on your gyro and used as a dipping sauce in much of the eastern Mediterranean for things like falafel and gyro meat. It is very easy to make at home, and cucumber can be added for additional freshness

## Equipment:

- Mixing bowl
- Cutting board
- Knife

## Ingredients

- .5 tablespoon of extra-virgin olive oil
- 7 ounces of whole fat Greek yogurt
- 1 clove of garlic
- Juice of .25 a lemon
- Dill

Directions:

1. Chop your garlic and dill finely.
2. Add yogurt, dill, olive oil, garlic, and lemon juice to the bowl. Cover.
3. Let sit overnight. Flavors are enhanced by doing so.

## Breakfast

This is the most important meal of the day, as wisdom decrees. Mediterranean diets tend to have simple breakfasts of just bread, oil, and a light protein, and many of these aren't codified here because of their simplicity. This obviously changes depending on personal preference, country, and, of course, hunger and skill level.

# Mediterranean toast

(535 kcal, P: 16 gr, Net Carbs: 56 gr, F: 28 gr, Fi: 5 gr)

This is a simple and hearty meal composed of foods from across the Mediterranean.

## Equipment:
- Toaster
- Cutting board
- Knife

## Ingredients:
- Salt and pepper
- 5 olives
- Tomato
- 1 tablespoon of olive oil
- 1 boiled egg
- Half Ciabatta roll

## Directions:
1. Slice egg into pieces, tomato in slices, and olives bisected.
2. Toast the bread until it looks nice and golden.
3. Pour oil over the bread slice, and top with egg, olives, tomatoes, and salt and pepper.

# Fisherman's Eggs

(410 kcal, P: 41 gr, F: 26 gr)

A hearty breakfast from those men who worked the docks, this breakfast is full of healthy fats, omega-3s, and protein to get you through the day.

**Equipment:**

- Spatula
- Cast iron pan
- Cutting board
- Knife

**Ingredients:**

- 1 clove of garlic
- 1 tablespoon of extra-virgin olive oil
- 1 can of sardines packed in olive oil
- 3 eggs

Directions:

1. Preheat oven to broil.
2. Heat the oil on a pan at medium-low. Meanwhile, smash and dice the garlic.
3. Once the oil is shiny, add garlic to the pan along with the drained can of sardines. Break them up and brown them.
4. Once the oven is heated, broil for 4 minutes.
5. Take the pan out of the oven, crack your three eggs in and stick her back in for three minutes.

6. Take out, scoop it off the pan, and serve on focaccia bread.

# Eggs in Purgatory

(250 kcal, P: 20 gr, Net Carbs: 7 gr, F: 15 gr, Fi: 2 gr)

A classic Italian dish that can be changed into the classic Moroccan version, with just the addition of some onion, chili, feta, and paprika.

**Equipment:**

- Pan with cover
- Cutting board (For shakshuka)
- Knife (Shakshuka)

**Ingredients:**

- 1 tablespoon of extra-virgin olive oil
- .5 cups of tomato sauce (See "mother" recipes)
- 3 eggs

**Directions:**

1. Heat sauce in a pan until bubbling, keep covered.
2. Make small wells in the sauce for the eggs. Add olive oil on the exposed parts.
3. Crack the eggs into the oil in the pan with the sauce.
4. Cover, turn heat to low and let poach for 5-8 minutes.

**To make shakshuka:**

1. Heat oil in a pan and finely dice the onion.
2. Add onion and chili flakes to the pan, mix in the tomato sauce.
3. Add a pinch of paprika.

4.  After the eggs are poached, add feta cheese and serve.

# Breakfast Salad

(180 kcal, P: 5 gr, Net Carbs: 8 gr, F: 10 gr, Fi: 2 gr per cup)

This is something like a milder version of a Greek salad, the same thing, but without the feta cheese and oregano, and with added spinach. This is a great healthy beginning to the day.

**Equipment:**

- Mixing bowl
- Spoon and fork
- Cutting board
- Knife

**Ingredients:**

- Salt and pepper
- Tablespoon of extra virgin olive oil and red wine vinegar
- 1 cucumber
- 1 tomato
- .5 cup of spinach

**Directions:**

1. Slice your cucumber in little coins, and cut them in half. Cut your tomatoes into quarters, and your spinach as fine as you can get it.
2. Throw these in your mixing bowl, dress with oil and vinegar, and season with salt and pepper.
3. Throw it in the fridge overnight to let the flavors really incorporate.

# Breakfast Frittata

(200 kcal, P: 10 gr, Net carbs: 10 gr, F: 12 gr, Fi: 2 gr per slice)

A frittata is a savory Italian egg-based casserole usually with vegetables, cheese, and meat. This a version featuring an energy rush for those busy mornings, but still with plenty of protein and healthy fat.

**Equipment:**

- Cast iron pan
- Spatula
- Cutting board
- Knife
- Whisk
- Bowl

**Ingredients:**

- Salt and pepper
- 1 clove of garlic
- 2 red potatoes
- Bundle of green onion
- Cheese for grating
- 6 eggs

**Directions:**

1. Preheat oven to 350.

2. Heat the oil the pan. Mince your garlic and green onions and potatoes. Fry the potatoes first until golden brown, and then add your garlic and onions.

3. Crack your eggs into a bowl while whisking and grating some cheese and adding the salt and pepper and oregano.

4. Once the vegetables are cooked, add eggs to the pan, and put uncovered in the oven until eggs are firm.

## Overnight Greek Oatmeal

(220 kcal, P: 9 gr, Net Carbs: 60 gr, F: 5 gr, and Fi: 7 gr)

There's an old quote about oatmeal; "Oats. A grain, which in England is generally given to horses, but in Scotland supports the people." I'm not sure if Greeks eat oatmeal. It always seemed like more of a northern European staple, but this fiber and energy-rich meal takes inspiration from their cuisine.

**Equipment:**

- Bowl
- Knife
- Cutting board
- Refrigerator

**Ingredients:**

- .3 cup of milk
- Pinch of cinnamon
- 3 dried figs
- Teaspoon of honey
- 3 dried dates
- .5 cups of oatmeal

Directions:

1. Chop your dried fruit into bits, set aside.
2. Combine your milk, splash of honey, fruit, and oatmeal, and mix thoroughly.
3. Throw it in the fridge for at least 8 hours.

4. When you open the fridge, it should be a solidified, semi-sweet, and rich porridge.

## Lunch

Lunches are usually light and casual affairs in this corner of the world, a quick break from work to refuel before getting back to whatever labor you were involved with. This is where pasta comes in – as it's easy to digest and quick to get down and provides you with a rush of energy. The diet's most questionable components, charcuterie, eaten for centuries also act as a protein of the poor.

# Pasta with Chili, Garlic, and Oil

(320 kcal, P: 7 gr, Net Carbs: 40 gr, F: 15 gr, Fi: 2 gr per cup)
Called "Pasta aglio e olio" in Italian - the most common pasta dish in Italy because of its taste and simplicity. Think of it as the Mediterranean equivalent to instant Ramen.

**Equipment:**

- Cutting board
- Knife
- Pot

**Ingredients:**

- Pasta (Spaghetti or other long pasta preferred)
- 1 garlic clove
- 1 tablespoon of olive oil
- Chili flakes

**Directions:**

1. Heat oil on medium-low. Meanwhile, smash garlic and cut fine.
2. Add chili to the oil once it's heated, then add your garlic clove. When your garlic is fragrant and lightly brown, it's done
3. Meanwhile, boil your pasta until al dente. Tender but not soft.
4. Strain the pasta, add back to the pot, and toss with garlic, oil, and chili.

5. Serve with either shredded parmesan or Romano cheese or Italian flat leaf parsley.

# Mediterranean Stuffed Chicken

(300 kcal, P: 43 gr, Net Carbs: 10 gr, F: 14 gr, Fi: 4 gr per breast)
This is chicken cordon bleu's thinner, more fibrous cousin. Not of any country in particular, but a mishmash of different flavors and textures.

**Equipment:**

- Frying pan
- Cutting board
- Knife
- Roasting pan
- Meat tenderizer

**Ingredients:**

- Salt and pepper
- Oregano
- 2 tablespoons extra virgin olive oil
- Chicken breast
- 1 Tomato
- 1 Zucchini
- 10 Black olives
- Red onion
- Feta cheese

Directions:

1. Preheat oven to 350 degrees Fahrenheit.

2. Butterfly the chicken breast and separate. Pound it as flat as you can with the tenderizer, set aside.

3. Finely slice all your vegetables in long, thin pieces. Divide your olives into fourths.

4. On your tenderized chicken, make slices against the grain and tuck your vegetables in. Season with salt, pepper, and oregano.

5. Heat olive oil in a pan of medium size.

6. Brown chicken briefly in the pan.

7. Take out of the pan. Put on a roasting pan and sprinkle with feta cheese.

8. Toss it in the oven, come back in 25 minutes.

9. Take out of oven, rest, and enjoy.

# Tortellini in broth with kale

(210 calories, P: 11 gr, Net Carbs: 33 gr, F: 5 gr, and Fi: 3 gr per 2 cups)

A famous soup from the north of Italy, and can be made extra delicious by using the recipe for the broth in the first section. It is comforting and warming on a winter's day, but also light enough to be enjoyed on-the-go.

## Equipment:

- Cutting board
- Knife
- Pan

## Ingredients:

- 1 tablespoon olive oil
- Oregano
- Rosemary
- Flat-leaf parsley
- Bundle of kale
- 1 onion
- 1 clove of garlic
- 1 lb of tortellini
- Bone stock

## Directions:

1. Heat olive oil on medium-low in the pan.

2. Smash and dice the garlic into fine pieces and dice onion finely.

3. Add onion, garlic, and rosemary to a pan, sweat until golden brown.

4. Add the stock and bring to a boil.

5. Boil the tortellini until al dente, and then add the oregano.

6. 2 or 3 minutes before the tortellini is finished, rip up the kale and parsley and let them boil in soup. When everything is soft and the tortellini rises to the top, the soup is complete.

# Tunisian Eggplant Salad

(290 kcal, P: 5 gr, Net Carbs: 12 gr, F: 24 gr, Fi: 5 gr per cup)

This is a recipe with probably a thousand variations around the Mediterranean, usually served cold or at room temperature with crusty bread. The eggplant absorbs the flavor of the oil and tomato very well, making this a decadent but guilt-free treat. It's sweet and sour and a good side or main course.

**Equipment:**

- Can opener
- Cutting board
- Knife
- Pot
- Colander

**Ingredients:**

- Salt and pepper
- 2 tablespoons of red wine vinegar
- 1 teaspoon of honey
- 3 Tablespoons of extra-virgin olive oil
- 1 onion
- 2 cloves of garlic
- 1 Eggplant
- 2 bell peppers
- Oregano
- 5 sage leaves

- Can of tomatoes, 15.5 ounces

Directions:

1. Heat oil in the pan to medium-low.
2. Slice the eggplant into discs and salt, put in a colander. (This keeps the eggplant from drinking up too much oil)
3. Slice the onions and garlic.
4. Add the onions and garlic to the pan.
5. Remove from the pan.
6. Slice the bell peppers into strips and add to the pan.
7. Remove from the pan once softened.
8. After 0.5 hours have passed, take the eggplant from the strainer and sauté in pan until soft.
9. Add tomatoes, onions, garlic, peppers, herbs, vinegar, and honey. Simmer until thickened.
10. Refrigerate overnight, serve cold.

## Pasta alla Norma

(320 kcal, P: 9 gr, Net Carbs: 49 gr, F: 10 gr, Fi: 5 gr per cup)
This is one of the national dishes of the island of Sicily – said to have been inspired by writer Nino Martoglio – who compared its delicate taste to the opera Norma, by Vincenzo Bellini.

**Equipment:**
- Cutting board
- Knife
- Pot
- Colander

**Ingredients**
- Salt and pepper
- 3 tablespoons extra-virgin olive oil
- 5 basil leaves
- Ricotta salata, parmesan, or pecorino romano
- 8oz of pasta – rigatoni works best.
- 1 eggplant
- 2 cups of tomato sauce

Directions:
1. Slice eggplant into discs, salt, and put in a colander to prevent it from drinking up too much oil.
2. After the time has passed, heat the oil in a pan of medium size. Add the eggplant and cook until soft.

3. Add tomato sauce to the eggplant and simmer until eggplant is tender.

4. Meanwhile, boil the water for the pasta and cook until it is al dente.

5. Just before serving, tear up basil leaves and add to the sauce pot.

6. Take pasta, dress with sauce, and grate some ricotta salata or other hard cheese on top.

## Stuffed Pita

(295 kcal, P: 18 gr, Net Carbs: 33 gr, F: 13 gr, Fi: 14 gr per whole pita)

A quick bite you can take with you on-the-go, this little pocket of nutrition supplies everything you need to keep you alert and focused so you aren't yelled at by your boss for passing out at work!

**Equipment:**

- Cutting board
- Knife
- **Ingredients**
- Juice of .25 lemon
- 1 Tomato
- .25 red onion
- 4 tablespoons of hummus
- .5 cups of spinach
- Boiled egg
- 2 oz crumble of feta cheese
- Whole pita

Directions:

1. Finely chop your onion, chop your tomato in slices, and cut your boiled egg into quarters
2. Open up your pita bread. Smear your hummus on both sides to work as a kind of "food glue."

---

3. Lay your spinach, then the tomato down, and top with your boiled egg quarters to weigh everything down.
4. Squeeze your lemon juice over it and lay your feta cheese on top and enjoy.

## Greek Salad

(180 kcal, P: 5 gr, Net Carbs: 8 gr, F: 10 gr, Fi: 2 gr per 160 grams)

The original greenless salad – the Salad that kept the men of Athens fighting Persia. It's delicious!

### Equipment:

- Cutting board
- Knife
- Mixing Bowl

### Ingredients

- Salt and pepper
- Savory
- Oregano
- 1 tablespoon of extra-virgin olive oil
- 1 tablespoon red wine vinegar
- cucumber
- Tomato
- .5 red onion
- 4 ounces of feta cheese

Directions:

1. Cut your cucumber into disks, tomato into fourths, and finely dice your onion.
2. Mix your oil and vinegar together.

3. Toss all your vegetables together. Pour your dressing over it. Season with oregano and savory, and crumble up your feta cheese on top of it.

# Roasted chickpeas

(255 kcal, P: 15 gr, Net Carbs: 47 gr, F: 1 gr, Fi: 11 gr)

Perfect for either a light lunch or a snack, these can be eaten with yogurt sauce (tzatziki) or with greens and rice.

## Equipment:

- Cutting board
- Pot
- Knife
- Roasting pan

## Ingredients

- 1 tablespoon extra-virgin olive oil
- Salt and pepper
- Onion
- .5 cup of dry chickpeas soaked for 8 hours or overnight
- Water or stock

Directions:

1. Heat olive oil on medium low.
2. Finely dice your onion and garlic, adding to the pan when the oil is hot.
3. Cook until brown, and then add your water or stock and chickpeas.
4. Simmer until the chickpeas are tender. Add salt and pepper.
5. Preheat oven to 350 degrees F.

6. Arrange the chickpeas with plenty of room on a roasting pan, and cook for 30 minutes or until crispy.

# Calabrese Salad

(220 kcal, P: 13 gr, Net Carbs: 5 gr, F: 17 gr, Fi: 1 gr per cup)

This is another greenless salad, this time coming from the "toe" of Italy, Calabria. Famous for its richness of flavor and fullness of ingredients, Calabrese can be an awesome lunch on its own.

## Equipment:

- Cutting board
- Knife

## Ingredients

- Salt and pepper
- 1 tablespoon of extra-virgin olive oil
- 1 tablespoon balsamic vinegar
- .5 lb of mozzarella
- 1 tomato
- 10 basil leaves

Directions:

1. Cut your tomato and mozzarella into 0.25 of inch slices.
2. Arrange them on a plate: tomato, basil leaf, and mozzarella.
3. Drizzle the top with balsamic vinegar and olive oil. Season with salt and pepper to taste.

# Mediterranean Wrap

(550 kcal, P: 34 gr, F: 22 gr, Net Carbs: 54 gr, Fi: 6 gr)

This is a modern invention with all the components of a good Mediterranean diet, from fibrous bread to lean protein to fresh vegetables. Carry one of these around with you and annoy everyone who asks how your burrito is by smugly responding you're having a Mediterranean wrap, THANK YOU VERY MUCH.

## Equipment

- Knife
- Cutting board

## Ingredients

- Salt and pepper
- .5 cup of chicken breast
- 2 ounces of feta cheese
- 1 tablespoon of hummus
- Juice of .25 lemon
- .5 of Cucumber
- .5 Tomato
- .25 Red onion
- .5 cups of spinach
- Tortilla wrap

Directions:

1. Finely dice your spinach and onion. Quarter your tomato, and cut your cucumber into discs.
2. Smear down your hummus, chopped vegetables, feta, and chicken into the tortilla and spray with lemon juice and season with salt and pepper.
3. Wrap like a burrito, pack up and eat.

Dinner

By necessity, dinners are hearty but not gut-destroying affairs in the Mediterranean. A day as a rural worker in this part of the world can be grueling, but the bounty of the earth will always provide them with enough energy to get up the next day and get their work done. Fish and chicken are common dinners, but occasionally, heavier roasts and stews are also not unknown.

# Pesce alla Ghiotta - Glutton's Swordfish

(220 kcal, P: 28 gr, Net Carbs: 6 gr, F: 14 gr, Fi: 1 gr per 100 grams)

While the name of this recipe may have you thinking you'll be packing on a gut, glutton in this context is a bit more delicate. It means someone who enjoys all the best things in life – but not necessarily in excess. It's a dish that's great for impressing company as well, so it would be a sure-fire hit for the next dinner party.

**Equipment:**

- Pan
- Cutting board
- Knife

**Ingredients (For three servings)**

- 1 tablespoon extra-virgin olive oil
- 1 tablespoon extra-lite olive oil
- Salt and pepper
- Oregano
- Marjoram
- Capers
- Chili flakes
- 10 olives
- 1 onion
- 1.5 cups of tomato sauce

- 1 lb of swordfish

**Directions:**

1. Dice your olives and onion as fine as possible.
2. Turn your pan on medium-high and fill with extra-lite olive oil.
3. Season the swordfish with salt and pepper.
4. Brown the swordfish on both sides and remove from pan.
5. Lower heat on the pan and add extra-virgin olive oil.
6. Add onion, chili, and olives to the pan and sweat until golden brown.
7. Add tomato sauce, oregano, marjoram, capers, and swordfish and let them cook until the swordfish falls apart easily when stabbed with a fork.

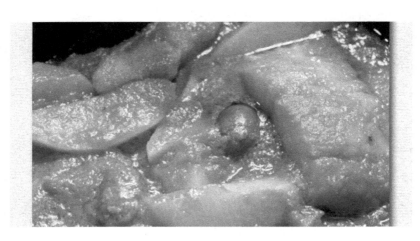

# Lemon Rosemary Roasted Chicken

(140 kcal, P: 14 gr, F: 9 gr for thigh meat; 366 kcal, P: 55 gr, F: 14 gr for breast) (180 kcal, P: 3 gr, F: 9 gr, Net Carbs: 23 gr, Fi: 3 gr for roasted vegetables)

Roasting a whole chicken can sometimes be something of an affair; or as I call it the 13th labor of Hercules. There's a decent amount of prep work involved but the results are usually worth it if everything goes as planned. The cut vegetables at the bottom work to keep the chicken from essentially boiling in its own juices.

**Equipment:**

- Cutting board
- Knife
- Mixing bowl
- Whisk
- Foil
- Roasting pan

**Ingredients**

- Salt
- Pepper
- Rosemary
- Juice of .5 lemon
- 2 red potatoes
- 1 carrot

- 1 onion
- 3 tablespoons of olive oil
- Whole chicken

**Directions:**

1. Preheat oven to 400.
2. Whisk together 2 tablespoons of oil, salt, pepper, lemon juice, and rosemary in a bowl.
3. Dice your vegetables into quarters, dressing with 1 tablespoon of olive oil, salt, pepper, and rosemary, and put in roasting pan.
4. Using a knife, separate chicken skin.
5. Pour oil under the skin of the chicken breast and leg.
6. Roast covered for 45 minutes.
7. Take it out, remove foil, and drop the heat to 350.
8. Put it back in for half an hour.
9. Take it out. If juice runs clear, it's cooked. If not, put it back in for 10 more minutes.
10. Let it rest for 15 minutes before carving, then serve.

## Pasta con le Sarde

Pasta with sardines may not sound particularly appealing if your palate is not so adventurous. But if treated right, this little canned fished can be astoundingly tasty contributors to a dish. This Italian classic is full of omega-3s, protein, and calcium.

(710 kcal, P: 28 gr, Net Carbs: 72 gr, F: 33 gr per half cup)

**Equipment:**

- Cutting board
- Knife
- 2 Pans

**Ingredients:**

- Anchovy paste
- Salt and pepper
- Red pepper flakes
- .5 lb of spaghetti
- 1 onion
- 2 cloves garlic
- 4 tablespoons of extra-virgin olive oil
- .25 a cup of white wine
- 2 cans of sardines, drained
- .25 cup of pine nuts
- .5 cup of bread crumbs

Directions:

1. Heat oil in a pan on medium-low. Dice your garlic and onions and add to pan.
2. As they soften, add red pepper flakes, anchovy paste, and sardines. Cook until brown.
3. Toast breadcrumbs in oil in a separate pan, and then put aside.
4. Meanwhile, boil water for pasta, cook al-dente.
5. Add wine to pan contents, add pine nuts and cook down for 10 more minutes.
6. Turn heat off, spoon sauce together with pasta and add bread crumbs as a topper.

## Greek Codfish

(200 kcal, P: 41 gr, F: 2 gr per 6 ounces)

This can be done either with salted, dried codfish that's been rehydrated or with a fresh cut. It's heavy on lemon and spices — the Greek way of doing things.

**Equipment:**

- Baking pan
- Knife
- Cutting board

**Ingredients:**

- 1 tablespoon extra-virgin olive oil
- Juice of .5 a lemon
- Salt and pepper
- Oregano
- Garlic powder
- Cumin
- .5 bundle Flat-leaf parsley
- 6-oz piece of codfish

**Directions:**

1. Preheat oven to 350.
2. Lay fish on a pan. Season with salt, pepper, half the lemon juice, parsley, cumin, garlic powder, and oregano.
3. Bake for 25 minutes or until crispy, taking out once at the 15-minute mark to pour the remaining lemon juice on.

4. Take fish out of the pan and let it rest for 10 minutes.

## Oregano Pork Loin

(325 kcal, P: 45 gr, F: 15 gr)

Pork loin is one of the more "aristocratic" meats – but can still be purchased cheaply if you know where to look. It's lean and full of protein. Because of this, it tends to dry out when grilled. That's why we're doing a dry brine, the longer the better.

### Equipment:

- Grill or broiler
- Roasting pan for broiler
- Grill tongs
- Meat Thermometer

### Ingredients

- .25 cup of salt
- Pepper
- 1 tablespoon of extra-virgin olive oil
- .25 cup of sugar
- 6oz of pork loin
- Oregano

### Directions:

1. Combine salt and sugar. Rub on pork with pepper and oregano and marinade for at least 8 hours. A day is best.
2. When ready to cook, get the grill heat to medium. Douse the loin piece with oil.

3. Grill, flipping once until the meat reads 160 degrees Fahrenheit. Check with a meat thermometer.

# Tunisian-Style Salmon

(410 kcal, P: 40 gr, F: 27 gr per 7 ounces)

Tunisia has been the home of many great civilizations over the past thousand years, namely the Phoenicians, Carthaginians, and the Umayyad Caliphate. They've long been a trading port – a place where you could get anything if you knew where to look. This reflects in the complexities of this dish.

## Equipment:

- Roasting pan
- Plastic bag
- Mortar and pestle or herb grinder

## Ingredients

- Salt and pepper
- .5 cup of flour
- Juice of 2 lemons
- 2 saffron threads
- 1 clove of crushed garlic
- Paprika
- Oregano
- Cumin
- Savory
- 7 ounces salmon fillet
- 6 tablespoons of extra-virgin olive oil

## Directions:

1. Grind saffron threads and dissolve in lemon juice.
2. Combine lemon juice, garlic, and olive oil in a bag with fish. Marinade for 8 hours or overnight.
3. Dredge the salmon in a mixture of salt and pepper, oregano, paprika, cumin, and savory.
4. Grill on 350, uncovered, until the fish flakes easily.

# Fasolada – Greek White Bean Soup

(310 kcal, P: 11 gr, Net Carbs: 39 gr, F: 14 gr, Fi: 8 gr)

For the average Hellenic, a dish more like this was probably far more common. It is made from things that could be grown easily and eaten cheaply, but still hearty enough to keep your belly from rumbling in the dead of night.

**Equipment:**

- Pot
- Cutting board
- Knife

**Ingredients:**

- Bay leaf
- 1 cup of white dry beans, soaked overnight
- 1 clove of garlic
- Salt and pepper
- 3 tablespoon extra-virgin olive oil
- 2 carrots
- 2 ribs of celery
- Tablespoon of tomato paste
- 1 onion
- Water (or bone stock)
- Paprika

**Directions:**

1. Heat olive oil to medium-low heat.

---

2. Dice all vegetables and garlic and add to pan. Cook until aromatic and brown.

3. Deglaze the pan with water or stock, stirring in tomato paste and bay leaf.

4. Pour in beans and increase heat to boil.

5. Let simmer until beans swell and are soft enough to eat.

# Spanish-Style Chicken Fricassee

(350 kcal, P: 30 gr, Net Carbs: 15 gr, F: 14gr, Fi: 4 gr per half cup)
Fricassee is a style of the dish with many different forms and
countries of origin, sort of like how the name sounds neither
100% Spanish nor French. This particular version is enriched
with beer – something not always commonly found in
Mediterranean cuisine but is used to excellent and delicious effect.

**Equipment:**

- Pot
- Cutting board
- Knife

**Ingredients:**

- Salt and pepper
- Bay leaf
- 1 onion
- Cumin
- 1 clove of garlic
- Whole chicken, cut up
- 3 tablespoons of extra-virgin olive oil
- 2 tablespoons of extra-lite olive oil
- 1 bottle of light beer
- 2 cans of crushed tomatoes
- 6 red potatoes
- 12-ounce jar of Spanish olives

Directions:

1. Season the chicken parts with salt and pepper. Pour lite olive oil into the pan and put on medium high.
2. Brown all the chicken parts and set aside.
3. Lower the heat and add extra-virgin olive oil.
4. Dice the garlic, onion, and carrot finely and add to the oil. Cook until brown and fragrant.
5. Add tomatoes, beer, spices, potatoes, and chicken.
6. Boil for 2 to 3 hours, or until chicken falls apart with a fork.
7. Serve with rice.

## Steak Pizzamaker's Style

(375 kcal, P: 36 gr, Net Carbs: 16 gr, F: 18 gr per 6 oz serving)

Pizzaiola – a pizzamaker in Naples, has a certain style of making a steak that is unusual, for most people, to say the least. Most people don't associate tomato sauce and steak, but this recipe melds the two excellently. This is best used with a tougher cut, like flank or brisket, but sirloin can serve just as well.

**Equipment:**

- 2 pans

**Ingredients**

- Salt and pepper
- 6 oz sirloin, flank, or brisket steak
- Oregano
- 1 tablespoon extra-lite olive oil
- 1 cup of tomato sauce

Directions:

1. Season your steak with salt, pepper, and oregano.
2. Meanwhile, get your tomato sauce simmering in the first pan.
3. Heat your extra-lite oil to high, and, when hot, sear your steak for 2 mins either side or until nicely browned.
4. Simmer in tomato sauce for 2-4 minutes and serve.

## Stuffed Tomatoes

(450 kcal, P: 29 gr, Net Carbs: 30 gr, F: 24 gr, Fi: 5 gr per tomato)
Otherwise known in Turkish as Domates dolmasi – stuffed
tomatoes are the rarer counterpart to the more often seen stuffed
peppers, but equally delicious. Also enjoyed by the Greeks, these
little flavor bombs have a reputation for being challenging, but all
they take is a little patience and they can be made easily.

**Equipment:**

- Roasting pan
- Pot
- Frying pan
- Cutting board

**Ingredients:**

- 8 tomatoes
- Salt and pepper
- 1lb ground meat
- Oregano
- 1 cup of rice
- Sage
- Thyme
- Onion
- 1 clove of garlic
- .5 cup of tomato sauce
- 2 tablespoons extra-virgin olive oil

Directions:

1. Preheat oven to 350. Warm oil in a pan to medium-low.
2. Put rice on a boil, starting on high heat, and reducing to medium once it starts to boil over.
3. Finely dice the onions and garlic and fry in oil until brown.
4. Add meat, oregano, sage, and cook until the meat is browned.
5. Meanwhile, cut the top of tomato off and scoop out the guts.
6. Once the rice and meat is cooked, mix it together, and stuff it inside a tomato
7. Put tomatoes on baking sheet and pour tomato sauce on top of it.
8. Put tomato top back on top and bake for 25 minutes.

## Chapter 6: Cultivation

Think of this as something like a little bonus to this book – and really, when you ponder over much of the material covered, it's no surprise that this would be an essential skill for those of us truly looking to dive into the diet as deeply as possible. This diet is one of the rural poor, who are farmers, by convention. These people always had fresh produce around the table, the star of many of their dishes, and they always knew how to grow their own food. This chapter only covers some of the basics, the easier vegetables, herbs, and fruits to grow, but hopefully, it's enough to get you started. You won't be milling your own flour or butchering your own cow, but at least you can taste your very own home-grown tomato, or at least stop having to buy basil at the grocery store every two weeks.

## Herbs

Starting with an herb garden is inherently less threatening than trying to grow a vegetable – it's where most people start with gardening because you're basically just growing some tasty weeds and sticks, something even those of us with no gardening inclination can do.

### Rosemary

"The Christmas herb," rosemary has a strong flavor and is extremely prevalent in many types of Mediterranean cuisine. It's not hard to grow, depending on where you live, and can soon grow to achieve the status of "obnoxious weed" if you're not too adamantly harvesting it.

There are two ways to grow rosemary – from seed or from a trimming. To get a quicker start, plant them indoors 9 weeks before your last frost. Once that's happened, plant them in well-drained, 70-degree soil with plenty of room to spread out, maybe three feet tall and three feet wide. When it flowers, trim it, and water enough to keep it moist but not swampy, maybe every other day. It needs full sun exposure to grow strong, and prune often to keep it from getting too skeletal. The younger the stems, the fresher the taste. They can be dried and used later.

## Basil

A plant that must grow like a weed in the Mediterranean – but a plant that I often fail to plant and harvest here. It comes in many varieties, lemony lemon basil (creative name!) the anise-like taste of Thai, and the milder purple basil. Good for making pesto, calabrese, or enhancing the flavor of tomato sauce, basil likes heat to stay healthy.

When planting, it likes full sun and soil temperature in between 50 and 70 degrees. It needs the warmth to grow, with 8 hours of sun a day. Shove them into the ground a foot apart, and 0.25 of an inch deep. Same with rosemary – enough water is needed to keep it moist, but don't drown the plant. It should be drained regularly. When it flowers, trim to keep your plant producing leaves, but, as it's an annual, it will die in a year. So, toward the latter end of its lifespan, let the flower seed to get a new generation of plant.

Bonus: Their favorite neighbors are tomatoes, which is cute, as they go so well together.

# Dill

Dill is a feathery-looking herb, commonly used in the eastern Mediterranean for soups and stews, and for pickling. It has the interesting effect of attracting certain helpful insects to your garden as well, predatory ones that drive off formican (ant) invaders and beetles. It also self-sows easily, so you can easily establish a permanent home for your herb.

Dill is also a full-sun plant. Interesting how all these Mediterranean plants need full sun! Keep the plants a foot and a half apart – and keep the soil warm, anywhere in the 60 to 70 degree-range. It does best when it's grown where it started. It does not tolerate transplanting and is somewhat frail – build a barrier so it's not knocked over by a strong wind. Water is best given every other day, and do not let flowers bloom on them. Within 20 to 30 days, some signs of dill should appear.

## Thyme

Thyme is a great plant for both seasoning and using as a source of puns. It has an herbal flavor akin to oregano or marjoram, but in a warmer, less intense way. It's a great seasoning for milder soups and stews, usually with chickens or beans as a starring ingredient. Thyme has a little more tolerance than the previous plants – you can plant it in the full or partial sun. It's cool with either, and it's a perennial, so it keeps coming back as long as you don't kill it. However, growing it from seeds can be a challenge. Try getting some from a friend in the form of clippings, and plant it 8 weeks before the last frost, and keeping the soil around 70 degrees. Keep it 8 inches away from its fellow sprigs, and water it every other day. Trim often and dry the sprigs in a dark area and store them airtight for continual use, or grind them into a powder.

## Italian/Curly Parsley

A cousin to the dill plant with bright leaves, parsley is a common addition as both a flavoring agent and a decoration to Mediterranean cuisine. It is an absolute essential for any garden and great for health. It is full of micronutrients, fiber, vitamins, and minerals.

Like thyme, this breed of parsley enjoys both full sun and partial sun and warm weather, about 70 degrees Fahrenheit optimally. Plant seeds in their own pots, in their own homes 10 weeks before the last frost. Soaking the seeds overnight gets them to grow a little easier. She's a bit of a slow starter, so waiting 3 to 4 weeks may be required, but it can handle cold weather, so don't get discouraged if it's been awhile. If planting together, give 8 inches of space. If you need extra light, a grow lamp about 2 inches above gives the plants the stimulation needed. Water as needed. Check the soil often for dryness.

Wait until all three "heads" of the leaf are grown in before harvesting, but trim from the outer area. Leave the inner part to mature. To keep the stalks lively, put the stalks in water in the fridge. Drying parsley can sometimes reduce flavor.

## Fruits and Vegetables

If you've managed to successfully grow a few of the things from the herb section, you're probably ready for a bigger challenge. Growing fresh produce can be intimidating, but give praise, we aren't working as sharecroppers, farmers, or, Zeus forbids, Neolithic agriculturalists. If we screw up, we can keep trying, – that's the key here, to keep trying. Growing vegetables can be frustrating to start with, but ultimately a very rewarding enterprise. We don't have the built-in knowledge of these farmer folks, but we have an infinite library of information to use at our leisure, so take advantage of it if there's something you want to grow.

### Cucumber

A casual, easy to grow vegetable that loves the sun and water, cucumbers respond well to constant watering and climbs up space easily. They also grow quickly for vegetables, and in relative abundance, leaving you with more pickles than you know what to do with. They also grow in containers quite easily, making them an option even for those of us trapped in apartments.

Again, they like full sun, and soil around 70 degrees. Plant them inside earlier, then move two weeks after the last frost as they need the heat. The soil is better if it is a little alkaline, around 7 on the pH scale. Mix manure down 8 inches deep and ensure the soil is not too soggy. Plant the buds 3 to 5 feet apart and an inch deep. They need constant watering, one inch a week. Put your finger in the dirt, and if it's dry an inch down, water it. When sprouts emerge, increase water to a gallon a week. Harvest them before they're too big for optimal taste, and not yellow. Keep the plant picked to keep it producing.

## Tomato

The perfect buddy to basil in the garden and the kitchen, a
tomato is easy for the first time gardener. Tomatoes are also
almost always better when picked fresh and local – supermarket
tomatoes are known for being lighter on flavor and on nutrients.
Consider pruning your plants earlier on for stronger-tasting fruits
with a better taste, but fewer plants overall. They need lots of
water and fertilizer in the form of eggshells or bone meal.
Start your tomatoes 6 to 8 weeks before the final frost to get
them a good head start, and water them well to keep the roots
healthy. They need full sun, and loose, well-drained soil. If doing
them in pots, one tomato per pot. Cherry tomatoes grow
exceptionally well in a pot. Keep your soil moist, and water it
extra in a heat wave. It needs 6 to 8 hours a day of full sun for
proper nourishment. Two inches of water a week to reach deep
down into the roots, and trim leaves 12 inches below the stem.
Leave them on the vine, let them ripen for as long as you can. If
any fall off before that, let them finish in a paper bag. Don't
refrigerate them either, keep them out in the open, and can be
kept in a sealed plastic bag, frozen.

## Zucchini

Zucchini is a famed vegetable because of their prolific nature —
they keep producing and producing and producing several per
day. That's why this is a good starter plant, it does good to
encourage the beginning farmer. They taste similar to their yellow
squash brethren, and are, in fact, simply their "winter squash"
equivalent, and can be used in a similar way, for noodles or in
roasts or stir-fries.

Start the seeds indoors, 3 weeks before the final cold snap of
spring, with soil hovering around 60 degrees Fahrenheit. Planting
it midsummer works well, too — you can avoid common pests and
blights that happen earlier in the growing season. They need lots
of compost and organic matter, egg shells, bone meal, that sort of
thing, so make sure it's properly woven into the soil ahead of
time. They like to be planted one-inch deep and about two feet
apart, and regular, weekly watering down into the root system is
needed. It is recommended to water them four inches down and
keep adding more organic matter into the dirt for optimal growth.
Zucchini is best harvested early on when they're small and still
tender to the touch for the best flavor. The larger the squash, the
more the flavors "spread out," weakening them. They average
two months to maturity, but once it gets going, you'll have
enough to be sick of them. It's recommended to cut the vine
instead of breaking it off.

## Spinach

Popeye's favorite is full of iron, fiber, and vitamins A and K, and is also one of the easier and rewarding leaves to start with. It's best to start in the early spring but needs a fed, rich soil. Tilling in manure would be best for this, about a week before you plant, and the second the ground thaws, the seeds are ready to go in the ground. The quicker the seeding the better.

Spinach needs full sun exposure, but the soil should not rise above 70 degrees. Plant your seeds half an inch deep and cover, and one seed per inch. Water regularly, and don't be afraid if it gets cold. Spinach tolerates temperatures as low as 20 degrees Fahrenheit. As or harvesting – it's mostly by eye. When do you think they look best? Then they're best, don't wait too long, as bitterness will settle into it quickly after maturity. Cut it off at its base, from the outer plants in to give the inner plants more time to reach maturity.

## Last words

Growing fruits, vegetables, and herbs is a rewarding hobby and an excellent addition to cooking and fits well with the protocol of the Mediterranean diet, but, it can be frustrating. As the beginning of the chapter said, start slow. Don't plant 10 different plants in 10 different ways and get frustrated and quit once they all die. Check them every day. Continual monitoring of their situation is the best way to asses their health and nip any problems in the bud before they start. Remember, too, that there are plenty of resources, from local gardeners and farmers in your area, to books, and the internet. Take advantage to maximize your growth potential, and to make your diet match its farmer origins as best it can.

# Conclusion

The Mediterranean is a big place. Dozens of different cultures and languages and cuisines blending together, but this, and its lush climate are part of the reason why it's such a culinary powerhouse today. It's a bounty for both the soul and the body, fit for a peasant or an emperor. Hopefully, this book carried you to wherever you wanted to be – whether that was health, performance, or simple curiosity.

This book was not intended to be the be-all end-all publication on Mediterranean food, but it was structured to serve as a knowledge basis – to give you a complete idea of the most basics of where to look when it came to making choices for yourself. Just the essentials and then enough to get you started, with enough to carry you in confidence. Hopefully, that happened, I had a drachma for every time I wrote: "olive oil, wine, bread, fish, I'd be hegemon by now". We also tried to give you a solid, calorie-precise guide to what you'll be eating, not so you can obsessively track every calorie, but so you can start thinking about the food choices you make every day in hopes that it will encourage you to find your way to a healthy lifestyle.

Changing your diet isn't a simple thing, but hopefully, we provided enough examples to inspire you on a culinary journey. Hopefully, you've gone on to integrate some aspects of the diet, or maybe you've made the full switch, or maybe find a new recipe you might like or encourage you to see *how bad are sardines really?* Cooking and eating is a fundamental part of existence, and it is also one of the most rewarding for the body and spirit. At the very least, we have enriched your life in the smallest way. Enjoy your meals with your friends and family to best effect, and don't be afraid to plant a seed. Whatever you've gleaned from this book, the one thing we must say is *Bon appetite!*

# Description

The Mediterranean diet is a powerful tool to transform your health and rabidly change your palate, and there's never been a better time to try something new. The diet has been in the works for over 2,000 years to reach its current and most perfect form for you! There are more options than ever, and the health benefits are still being elucidated, but they include things like:

- Reduce the severity of obesity.
- Better control over heart disease – lowering bad cholesterol and dropping blood pressure.
- Eliminate metabolic syndrome, effectively eliminating diabetes before it starts
- Cancer prevention

How does this work? You ask in amazed wonder. I reply – "A diet high in polyphenols, an anti-inflammatory antioxidant found in foods such as olive oil, fish, and vegetables, all of which are present in high numbers in this diet!" Which receives an eye of curiosity for the uncalled information dump. The point is the diet is very rich in certain foods very high in antioxidants, healthy fats, and fiber, all of which are thoroughly lacking in modern-day Western diets. There are a trio and its two hangers on to thanks for this, which have been espoused by writers and historical figure for their vitality-giving powers. They are the olive, the grape, and wheat. Olive oil, wine, and bread. And then the two hangers-on are the primary protein; fish, high in omega-3s, and the richness of vegetables, present in almost every meal no matter the occasion. All research corroborates that this is food the body thrives on. You grumble, in your modern incarnation, recalling your past life as a degenerate Athenian, maybe that Hippocrates ingrate was on to something.